BMX RACING

APEX

BY HUBERT WALKER

WWW.APEXEDITIONS.COM

Apex is distributed by North Star Editions:
sales@northstareditions.com | 888-417-0195

Produced for Apex by Red Line Editorial.

Photographs ©: Shutterstock Images, cover, 1, 4–5, 6, 7, 8–9, 10–11, 12–13, 14, 15, 16–17, 18, 19, 20, 21, 22–23, 24–25, 26, 27, 29

Library of Congress Control Number: 2021915725

ISBN
978-1-63738-150-2 (hardcover)
978-1-63738-186-1 (paperback)
978-1-63738-256-1 (ebook pdf)
978-1-63738-222-6 (hosted ebook)

Printed in the United States of America
Mankato, MN
012022

NOTE TO PARENTS AND EDUCATORS

Apex books are designed to build literacy skills in striving readers. Exciting, high-interest content attracts and holds readers' attention. The text is carefully leveled to allow students to achieve success quickly. Additional features, such as bolded glossary words for difficult terms, help build comprehension.

TABLE OF CONTENTS

CHAPTER 1

RACE DAY

The starting gate drops down. BMX riders speed down a steep hill. Next, they fly over several big jumps.

Eight riders usually compete in a BMX race.

The riders race around the first turn. Two riders bump into each other. They crash to the ground. The other riders keep pedaling.

In BMX racing, the turns are called berms.

Crashes are a dangerous part of BMX racing.

BMX tracks often have several small bumps in a row. These bumps are called rollers.

TILTED TURNS

Most crashes happen on the track's turns. Each turn's edges **slant** upward. Riders tilt sideways as they go around it. This helps them keep their speed.

The riders fly over more jumps. They go around more turns. Then they race to the finish line. The winner raises a fist in victory.

Most BMX races last for 30 to 40 seconds.

BMX tracks can feature several kinds of jumps.

CHAPTER 2

HISTORY OF BMX RACING

Kids invented BMX racing in the 1960s. They wanted to act like **motocross** riders. In fact, BMX is short for "bicycle motocross."

Motocross riders use motorcycles that can handle rough dirt tracks.

BMX races happen all over the world.

In the 1970s, a group made official rules for BMX racing. The first world **championship** took place in 1982.

BMX racers can reach speeds of more than 35 miles per hour (56 km/h).

BMX racing continued to gain popularity in the 1990s. Riders from all over the world took part. In 2008, BMX racing became an Olympic sport.

The 2008 Olympic Games took place in Beijing, China.

Beijing 2008

BMX racers compete in the 2016 Olympic Games in Rio de Janeiro, Brazil.

BMX FREESTYLE

BMX freestyle is a similar sport. Bikers compete by doing tricks. They jump, flip, and spin. Some bikers use ramps, rails, or other **obstacles**. Others do tricks on flat ground.

CHAPTER 3

RACING RULES

The rules of BMX racing are simple. Riders must stay in their **lanes** for the first few feet. After that, they just have to stay on the track.

Most BMX tracks are 900 to 1,300 feet (274–396 m) long.

BMX racing can be a rough sport. Riders often crash into one another. But it's against the rules to force others off the track.

Having eight bikes on a narrow track means that racers often ride very close to one another.

Learning to stick landings is one tough part of BMX.

On some jumps, riders can go nearly 16 feet (5 m) high.

The youngest BMX racers ride bikes known as striders.

BMX races are divided by age and gender. They are also divided by skill level. Beginners and expert riders take part in different races.

REACHING THE FINALS

BMX races have several **rounds**. Riders get points for how well they do. Only the best riders make it to the final round.

A BMX racer competes in a women's race in Russia.

CHAPTER 4

BMX EQUIPMENT

The bike is the most important piece of equipment in BMX racing. Bike **frames** are made of light metal. Most BMX bikes have 20-inch (51-cm) wheels.

BMX bikes are smaller than other kinds of bikes.

Bikes with larger wheels tend to be easier to ride.

Some BMX bikes have 24-inch (61-cm) wheels. These bikes are known as cruisers. They race in their own **category**.

BUILDING LIGHTER BIKES

Riders can go faster if their bikes don't weigh as much. So, companies often make their bikes as light as possible. Many racing bikes are made of a light metal called chromoly.

Safety gear is important in BMX racing. Riders must wear helmets and gloves. They must also wear long-sleeve shirts and long pants.

Helmets help keep riders' heads safe during races.

Pro BMX racers often have company logos on their safety gear.

Many riders wear knee pads and shin guards for extra safety.

COMPREHENSION QUESTIONS

Write your answers on a separate piece of paper.

1. Write a sentence that explains the main idea of Chapter 2.

2. What do you think is the most exciting part of a BMX race? Why?

3. When was BMX racing invented?

    A. 1960s

    B. 1970s

    C. 1990s

4. Why are BMX races divided by skill level?

    A. to make sure riders won't go too fast

    B. to make sure crashes do not happen

    C. to make sure races are as fair as possible

5. What does **popularity** mean in this book?

*BMX racing continued to gain **popularity** in the 1990s. Riders from all over the world took part.*

   A. when something is liked by many people
   B. when people are able to move
       very quickly
   C. when very few people enjoy something

6. What does **expert** mean in this book?

*They are also divided by skill level. Beginners and **expert** riders take part in different races.*

   A. unsure of one's ability
   B. very good at something
   C. not able to perform well

Answer key on page 32.

GLOSSARY

category
A group of races for riders of a certain age, vehicle, or skill level.

championship
A contest that decides a winner.

frames
The metal parts that give bikes their shape. A bike's seat, pedals, and wheels attach to the frame.

lanes
Areas on a track where racers must ride. Each lane is bordered by stripes.

motocross
A type of motorcycle racing that takes place on dirt tracks.

obstacles
Things that block a rider's way.

rounds
Races that take place in the earlier parts of a contest. These races decide who moves on to the finals.

slant
To tip so that one side is higher than the other.

TO LEARN MORE

BOOKS

Chandler, Matt. *Chad Kerley: BMX's Breakout Star*. North Mankato, MN: Capstone Press, 2021.

Hudak, Heather C. *BMX*. New York: AV2 by Weigl, 2021.

Koehn, Rebecca. *BMX*. Minneapolis: Abdo Publishing, 2021.

ONLINE RESOURCES

Visit **www.apexeditions.com** to find links and resources related to this title.

ABOUT THE AUTHOR

Hubert Walker enjoys running, hunting, and going to the dog park with his best pal. He grew up in Georgia but moved to Minnesota in 2018. Overall, he loves his new home, but he's not a fan of the cold winters.

INDEX

Answer Key:
1. Answers will vary; **2.** Answers will vary; **3.** A; **4.** C; **5.** A; **6.** B